Let's Talk About
BEING LAZY

Let's Talk About
BEING LAZY

By JOY BERRY

Illustrated by John Costanza
Edited by Orly Kelly
Designed by Jill Losson

GROLIER ENTERPRISES CORP.

Let's talk about BEING LAZY.

Have people ever asked you to do something for them that they could have done for themselves?

Has someone not helped you when you needed help?

Sometimes people will ask you to do something because they are too *lazy* to do it for themselves.

Sometimes people will not help you because they are too *lazy* to help.

When someone is being lazy around you —

- how do you feel?
- what do you think?
- what do you do?

When someone is being lazy around you —

- you may feel frustrated and angry;
- you may think it's too much work to be around the person;
- you may choose not to stay around him or her.

It is important to treat other people the way you want to be treated.

If you do not want other people to be lazy around you, you should not be lazy around them.

If you do not want to be lazy, *take care of yourself.*

Do not ask anyone to do anything for you that you can do for yourself.

For example, if you need something that you can get for yourself, don't ask someone else to get it for you.

You can also take care of yourself by doing these things:

- Keep yourself clean. Take a bath, wash and comb your own hair, and brush your own teeth.
- Dress yourself. Decide what clothes you are going to wear and put them on by yourself.

If you do not want to be lazy, *clean up after yourself.*

- Keep your bedroom orderly. Keep everything in it picked up.
- Help keep your house neat. Put things away after you use them.
- Clean up any mess you make.

If you do not want to be lazy, *be helpful.*

Help out by doing small jobs around your house. Here are just a few things you could do:

- Set the table for meals.
- Clean the table after meals.
- Do the dishes.
- Empty the trash.

Can you think of more things you could do to help out around your house?

Taking care of yourself, cleaning up after yourself, and helping out may not always be fun. Sometimes these things are work.

Try to be a good sport about your work.
- Don't complain about it.
- Don't wait to be reminded to do it.
- Don't try to get out of doing it.
- Don't put it off until later.

To make your work more fun, you may want to do these things:

- *Play a game with yourself.* Set yourself a time limit and try to get the job done in that amount of time.

- *Reward yourself.* Promise yourself that you will do something you really want to do after you finish your job. Be sure to keep the promise you make to yourself.

If you—

  · · · take care of yourself,

  · · · clean up after yourself, and help out,

you will not be lazy. This will make the people around you happy. It will also help you to become a better person.